YOUR KNOWLEDGE HAS VALUE

AF140759

- We will publish your bachelor's and master's thesis, essays and papers

- Your own eBook and book - sold worldwide in all relevant shops

- Earn money with each sale

Upload your text at www.GRIN.com
and publish for free

Bibliographic information published by the German National Library:

The German National Library lists this publication in the National Bibliography; detailed bibliographic data are available on the Internet at http://dnb.dnb.de .

Imprint:

Copyright © 2016 GRIN Verlag, Open Publishing GmbH
Print and binding: Books on Demand GmbH, Norderstedt Germany
ISBN: 9783668377233

This book at GRIN:

http://www.grin.com/en/e-book/350729/performance-evaluation-of-processors-with-caches

Alexander Mircescu

Performance Evaluation of Processors with Caches

GRIN Publishing

GRIN - Your knowledge has value

Since its foundation in 1998, GRIN has specialized in publishing academic texts by students, college teachers and other academics as e-book and printed book. The website www.grin.com is an ideal platform for presenting term papers, final papers, scientific essays, dissertations and specialist books.

Visit us on the internet:

http://www.grin.com/

http://www.facebook.com/grincom

http://www.twitter.com/grin_com

Performance Evaluation of Processors with Caches

Dr. Alexander Mircescu, Munich, Germany

Content

The processor performance influences the performance of the whole communication network. The available bandwidth of the processor determines the number of Busy Hour Call Attempts (BHCA) which can be processed by the communication network [1].

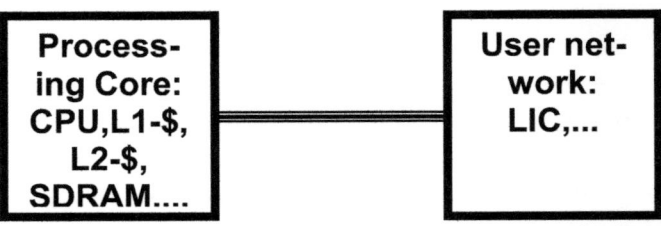

Figure 1: Coupling of processor and user network

Figure 1 illustrates how both subsystems are coupled by the communication bandwidth between them. Considering the elements of the processing core (MPU) like CPU, caches, main memory, etc. and the application a maximal call bandwidth B_{Call} can be offered to the user network. Dependent on the mean message length $\overline{l_{Call}}$ of a call the maximal call frequency f_{Call} can be computed [1]:

$$B_{Call} = \overline{l_{Call}} \cdot f_{Call}$$

In the following sections the influence the caches regarding the speedup is investigated.

1. Evaluation of the access characteristics

By analysis of the trace of a typical application the accessed addresses can be evaluated [1]. This result is dependent on the combination "hardware architecture-compiler"; therefore if several combinations are utilized several traces have to be evaluated [1].

2. Parameters influencing the cache hit rate

2.1 Performance measurement criteria

The scope of this list is to define orthogonal criteria which characterize the type of the application with respect to the processing performance. The criteria can be divided into two different categories: *spatial* and *temporal*. Spatial criteria are based on the properties of the address space utilized by the application; temporal criteria describe the behavior of the application with all it's modules in time. (The division in space and time is motivated by the functionality of the processor-bus-memory system which determines the performance of the application. The access of the processor via the bus system to it's instructions and data in the memory is realized with physical addresses. Therefore the knowledge and consideration of dependencies of addresses utilized by the application influences the performance. Additionally the distribution of the required addresses in time determines the performance.) Both criteria categories apply for data and instructions in the same way.

Spatial (code and data)	Temporal (code and data)
Spatial continuity (spatial reference locality): how many adjacent addresses are executed until a jump comes? *(deep <u>loops</u> can best be exploited by big cache lines)*	**Temporal continuity (temporal reference locality)**: how many time units (processor clocks) is the same <u>address</u> executed? *(a long duration can best be exploited by many cache lines)*
Spatial discontinuity: how long are the address jumps? *(long <u>if-then-else</u> generated jumps are best exploited by a high associativity)*	**Temporal discontinuity**: how long are the time periods between the <u>reuse</u> of the same address? *(long periods are best exploited by many cache lines)*
Spatial isolation: how big are address spaces which are <u>never used</u> during application? *(big spaces are best exploited by a high associativity)*	**Temporal isolation**: how big are time periods where the processor does <u>not access</u> the cache? *(long periods are best exploited by a high associativity)*
Spatial isolation frequency: <u>how many</u> address isolations occur? *(many isolations are best exploited by a high associativity)*	**Temporal isolation frequency**: <u>how often</u> do temporal isolation occur? *(high frequencies are best exploited by a high associativity)*
Interrupt distribution: how are the <u>interrupt addresses</u> distributed in address space? *(a wide distribution can be best exploited by a high associativity and random replacement strategy)*	**Interrupt frequency**: how <u>often</u> do <u>interrupts</u> occur? *(high frequencies can best be exploited by high associativity and random replacement)*

Table 1: Spatial and temporal criteria

Every application always consists of a combination of all described spatial and temporal criteria. The weight of each criterion regarding the performance influence is determined by it's frequency of occurrence and thus varies from one application to another. The estimation of the actual weights can be roughly proceeded by functional analysis of the application. But a precise determination of the parameters can only be obtained by trace evaluation. The same reasoning applies for data and instructions.

The following figure 2 gives a graphical representation of the processor access characteristics using a spacetime diagram. The green arrows and points represent all addresses accessed by the processor during operation time. Inclined arrows represent cases where the processor accesses a series of adjacent addresses (loop execution) and can be viewed as movements in the address space. The length of the inclined green arrow is proportional to the spatial continuity. Vertical arrows show repeated (adjacent) accesses to the same address and can be viewed as resting points in address space. The length of the vertical green arrow is proportional to temporal continuity. Green points finally represent one single access to one address implying no access to the adjacent address; they can be viewed as single disconnected events.

Red dotted arrows show jumps in address space occurring during execution of the program. The length of the red arrow is proportional to the spatial discontinuity. Brown dotted vertical arrows describe non-adjacent accesses to the same address between different green arrows or series of green arrows encoding the temporal discontinuity. Finally blue dotted horizontal and vertical arrows represent address ranges never accessed by the processor and time intervals at which the processor does not access the cache respectively. (Note that the blue dotted arrows can be transformed to a blue point if the address range or time interval equals 1. This case is not described in figure 2 because it leads to no deeper understanding.) The length of the horizontal blue arrow is proportional to the spatial isolation whereas the length of the vertical blue arrow is proportional to the temporal isolation. Note that green points are always surrounded by red and/or blue dotted arrows underlining their effect of strong spatial and temporal discontinuity decreasing the cache hit rate. The number of horizontal and vertical dotted blue arrows equals the spatial isolation frequency and the temporal isolation frequency respectively.

Interrupts are always causing spatial and temporal discontinuities so they are coupled to red dotted lines. It is not possible, however, to distinguish in the spacetime diagram if the jumps occur due to interrupts or not. Therefore the interrupt distribution and interrupt frequency cannot be read out of figure 2; or in other words: the cause of the jumps is not encoded in the figure.

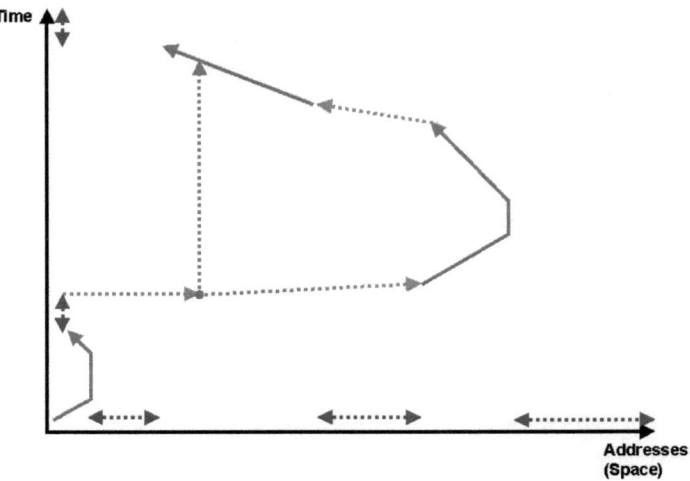

Figure 2: Spacetime diagram

The measurement of the spatial and temporal criteria can be realized in a simple way. Each trace contains the addresses accessed during operation thus allowing the analysis of all spatial criteria. Further it is possible to adjust a time stamp to each address in the trace defining the point in time when the address was accessed; evaluating the time stamp information one obtains all temporal criteria.

2.2 Performance influencing cache parameters

The obtained trace file is read by the cache simulator and the cache hit rate is computed. The cache hit rate depends on the parameters [1]:

- Cache line size
- Cache size
- Associativity
- Unified or non-unified cache
- Cache refill strategy

Some comments:

1. The cache line size is greater than the length of a processor information unit (byte, half word, word or double word) and is filled using the corollary of spatial reference locality [1]. Example: if the processor information unit is 64 bit and the cache line is 64 byte then 8 different processor information units can be stored in one cache line. The filling of the cache line with processor information units is realized with the help of the corollary of spatial reference locality: the first information unit is chosen on the request of the processor. As the following information unit the nearest neighbor in the address space is chosen and so on. This mechanism uses obviously the corollary of spatial reference locality. For applications with a great spatial reference locality (e. g. deep loops) a deep cache line is therefore of greatest importance.

2. The number of cache lines is of great importance regarding the temporal reference locality because the mechanism for the replacement of a cache line by another uses the corollary of temporal reference locality [1]. This is understood as follows: it is expected that the processor information unit which was demanded by the processor will be later demanded again. Therefore information which was loaded into a cache line remains there until the processor demands another information unit which has to be mapped to the same cache line. For applications with a great temporal locality (e.g. frequent call of a procedure) a high number of cache lines is of great importance and advantage.

3. The associativity is a parameter being important for the efficient usage of the temporal reference locality [1]. This can be understood as follows: in a direct mapped cache one line of the main memory is mapped to exactly one cache line. Therefore the possible values of each cache line are limited as given by the quotient

    $$Number-of-pos.-val.-of-a-cache-lin. = \frac{Number-of-main-mem.-lin.}{Number-of-cache-lin.}.$$ If

    the temporal reference locality of the actual application is quite small then the cases increase where two (or even more) main memory lines which are often called by the processor are replacing each other in the same cache line thus increasing the access time to the memory and decreasing the overall system performance. With increasing associativity this negative effect can be decreased due to the fact that each memory line can be placed to different cache lines (the number of possibilities increases with the grade of associativity and equals the number of cache lines for a full associative cache). The increasing freedom of placement to different cache lines increases the possibilities for the avoidance of the effect of alternative replacement of often used main memory lines in the same cache line. In summary it can be concluded that the performance loss due to a small temporal reference locality can be compensated by an increasing degree of associativity.

4. The implementation of a cache as separate data and instruction cache or as unified cache has (dependent on the application) also impact on cache hit rate and therefore also on the overall system performance [1]. In an unified cache a high temporal reference locality of instructions can lead to a very high occupation grade of the cache by the instructions decreasing the cache hits for the data access (or vice versa) and therefore possibly decreasing the overall system performance. Additionally a separate data and instruction cache offers a double communication bandwidth to the processor in comparison to a unified cache. Especially for large caches with smaller hit rates (level 2 caches) the implementation of unified caches is appropriate due to a small replacement effect between data and instructions and a matching of the needed and offered communication bandwidth between processor and cache.

5. The simplest cache refill strategy is given by the method "last recently used" [1]. This method is based on the measurement of the temporal reference locality of the accesses to the associative cache using a buffer where access information is stored. The LRU (last recently used)-logic analyses this information and decides which cache line of the actual set shall be replaced. In principle the LRU-unit can be based on a more complex functionality evaluating also spatial reference locality and/or trying to predict the optimal set for replacement. The implementation of a specific LRU-logic differs in many cases from processor to processor; its precise specification being sometimes difficult to obtain. The impact of the LRU-strategy on the performance varies from application to application.

6. *Summary of the points 1-5*: The cache line size and the number of cache lines are most important regarding the optimal utilization of the spatial and temporal reference locality of data and instructions. Therefore the trace-based evaluation of the reference locality is of great importance for the decision towards an appropriate cache. The associativity grade, the replacement strategy and the way of implementation (separate or unified) also influence the overall performance but in most applications in a smaller amount and are therefore omitted here.

2.3 Performance influencing application properties

The performance measurement criteria described earlier can be utilized to achieve quantitative predictions regarding the cache hit rate and thus regarding the performance of the processor. We make following definitions:

- Spatial continuity V: $V = \dfrac{\sum\limits_{i=1}^{n}|v_i|}{n}$. The v_i are represented by the inclined green arrows of figure 2. The variable n equals the number of inclined green arrows in figure 2.

- Spatial discontinuity W: $W = \dfrac{\sum\limits_{i=1}^{m}|w_i|}{m}$. The w_i are represented by the red dotted arrows of figure 2. The variable m equals the number of red dotted arrows in figure 2.

- Spatial isolation Ω: $\Omega = \dfrac{\sum\limits_{i=1}^{l}|\omega_i|}{l}$. The ω_i are represented by the blue horizontal dotted arrows of figure 2. The variable l equals the number of blue horizontal dotted arrows in figure 2.

- Temporal continuity T: $T = \dfrac{\sum\limits_{i=1}^{k}|t_i|}{k}$. The t_i are represented by the vertical green arrows of figure 2. The variable k equals the number of vertical green arrows in figure 2.

- Temporal discontinuity U: $U = \dfrac{\sum\limits_{i=1}^{j}|u_i|}{j}$. The u_i are represented by the brown dotted arrows of figure 2. The variable j equals the number of brown dotted arrows in figure 2.

- Temporal isolation Θ: $\Theta = \dfrac{\sum\limits_{i=1}^{h}|\vartheta_i|}{h}$. The ϑ_i are represented by the blue vertical dotted arrows of figure 2. The variable h equals the number of blue vertical dotted arrows in figure 2.

- Number of cache lines: ζ

- Length of cache line in bit: ξ

- Cache hit rate: χ

We further make following assumptions.

Spatial part:
1. ξ is proportional to $\chi_{Spatial}$ and ξ is proportional to V ➔ ξ is proportional to $\chi_{Spatial}$ V
2. ξ is proportional to $\chi_{Spatial}$ and ξ is proportional to 1/W ➔ ξ is proportional to $\chi_{Spatial}$ /W
3. According to 1 and 2: ξ is proportional to $\chi^2_{Spatial}$ V/W

4. According to 3 we can write the formula: $\chi_{Spatial} = K_1 \sqrt{\xi \dfrac{W}{V}}$.

Temporal part:

1. ζ is proportional to $\chi_{Temporal}$ and ζ is proportional to T ➔ ζ is proportional to $\chi_{Temporal}$ T
2. ζ is proportional to $\chi_{Temporal}$ and ζ is proportional to 1/U ➔ ζ is proportional to $\chi_{Temporal}$ /U
3. According to 1 and 2: ζ is proportional to $\chi^2_{Temporal}$ T/U
4. According to 3 we can write the formula: $\chi_{Temporal} = K_2 \sqrt{\zeta \dfrac{U}{T}}$.

Considering both parts (spatial and temporal) we can formulate:

1. The cache hit rate χ is proportional to $\chi_{Spatial}$ and is proportional to $\chi_{Temporal}$ ➔ χ is proportional to $\chi_{Spatial}\chi_{Temporal}$

2. According to 1 we can write the formula: $\chi = K \sqrt{\xi \zeta \dfrac{WU}{VT}}$, with K=K$_1K_2$.

The magnitudes W, U, V and T have to be determined by the trace evaluation, implementing counters in the trace evaluator. ζ and ξ are dependent on the used processor. The constant K has to be determined by experiments. The influence of the spatial isolation Ω and temporal isolation Θ regarding the cache hit rate is smaller for most applications than that of W, U, V, T and is therefore not considered here. Also the influence of the associativity of the cache, of the replacement strategy and the implementation as separate data-instruction-cache or as unified cache are regarded as small enough to be omitted in our approximate calculations.

3. Computation of the performance gain

In this section we analyze the performance gain which can be obtained by the reduction of the average memory access time realized by the utilization of caches [1].

3.1 Average memory access time

The average memory access time is determined by two main aspects: the physical access time to the memory which is dependent on the physical structure of the memory (DRAM, SRAM or FEPROM) and the functional access time which is dependent on the memory organization (e. g. caches) [1]. In the following subsections we concentrate on three different cases: a system with DRAM main memory and no cache, a system with DRAM main memory and level 1 cache and finally a system with DRAM main memory, level 1 and level 2 cache.

3.1.1 No cache

For a system with no cache we obtain the equation [1]:

$$t_{acc1} = t_{DRAM}$$

The variable t_{acc1} describes the average access time to the memory. If no cache is available this time is equivalent to the access time to the DRAM main memory t_{DRAM}. t_{DRAM} is dependent on the speed of the memory bus (e.g. SDRAM-bus) and the DRAM access time and can be extracted from the manual of the utilized DRAM-memory-type (e.g. SDRAM-manual). For a 500 MHz processor (5 ns cycle time) a possible value for t_{DRAM} can be 50 cycles (250 ns).

3.1.2 Level 1 cache

For a system with a level 1 cache the average access time to the memory is equal to [1]:

$$t_{acc2} = t_{HitL1} + f_{MissL1} t_{DRAM}$$

The variable t_{acc2} describes the average access time to the memory. In the case of a cache we must consider two cases: the data is read from the cache or from the main memory. The cases where it is fetched from the cache are represented by the first summand (t_{HitL1} describes the access time to the level 1 cache if a cache hit occurs). The second summand depicts the cases where due to a cache miss the data has to be fetched from the main memory (f_{MissL1} describes the miss rate of the level 1 cache). Possible values of the equation components are (for a 500 MHz processor) one tact cycle (5 ns) for t_{HitL1} and 50 cycles (250 ns) for t_{DRAM}. The miss rate depends on the application and therefore can show large variations (in many applications the miss rate is about 3 %).

3.1.3 Level 1 and level 2 cache

Finally for a system with a level 1 and a level 2 cache the average memory access time is equal to [1]:

$$t_{acc3} = t_{HitL1} + f_{MissL1}(t_{HitL2} + f_{MissL1L2} \, t_{DRAM})$$

The variable t_{acc3} describes the average access time to the memory. Here we have to distinguish between three cases.

1. The data is read from the level 1 cache. In this case the access time equals t_{HitL1}.
2. The date has to be read from the level 2 cache. In this case the access time is the product of the miss rate for the level 1 cache (f_{MissL1}) and the access time to the level 2 cache (t_{HitL2}).
3. The data must be read from main memory. In this case the access time equals the product of the miss rate for the level 1 cache (f_{MissL1}), the miss rate for the level 2 cache ($f_{MissL1L2}$) and the access time to the DRAM (t_{DRAM}).

$f_{MissL1L2}$ is obtained as follows. If from 100 accesses to the memory 80 lead to a hit in the level 1 cache then $f_{MissL1} = 20\%$. If from this remaining 20 accesses 10 lead to a hit in the level 2 cache then $f_{MissL1L2} = 50\%$. So generally spoken $f_{MissL1L2}$ is:

$$f_{MissL1L2} = \frac{Number-of-misses-in-the-level-2-cache}{Number-of-accesses-to-the-level-2-cache}$$

For a 500 MHz processor possible values of the equation components are: 1 tact cycle for t_{HitL1} (5 ns), 10 cycles for t_{HitL2} (50 ns) and 50 cycles for t_{DRAM} (250 ns). f_{MissL1} and $f_{MissL1L2}$ are dependent on the application and can widely vary (in many computer applications we have $f_{MissL1} = 3\%$ and $f_{MissL1L2} = 20\%$).

3.1.4 Level 1, level 2 and level 3 cache

For three levels of cache we obtain the formula:

$$t_{acc4} = t_{HitL1} + f_{MissL1}[t_{HitL2} + f_{MissL1L2}(t_{HitL2} + f_{MissL1L2L3} t_{DRAM})]$$

3.1.4 *n* levels of cache

$$t_{acc(n+1)} = \sum_{\alpha=1}^{\alpha=n+1} t_\alpha \left(\prod_{\beta=0}^{\beta=\alpha-1} f_\beta \right)$$

For *n* levels of cache we obtain the formula:

The variable f describes the miss-rate in the cache. We have $f_0=1$; f_i describes the miss-rate in the i-th level of cache. The variable t describes the access time to the cache. t_i describes the access time to the i-th level of cache; $t_{(n+1)}$ describes the access time to the main memory (DRAM).

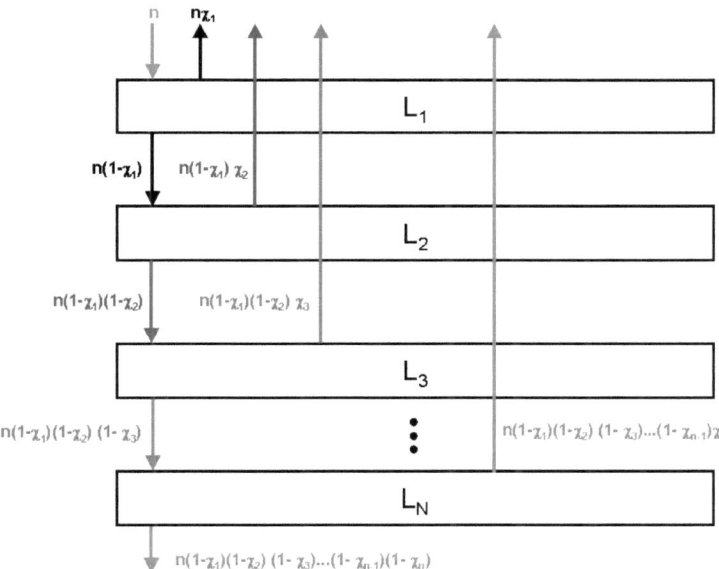

Figure 3: Accesses to N levels of cache (n: number of processor accesses to the level 1 cache)

3.2 CPU-time

The CPU-time can be obtained as follows [1]:

$$CPU_i = IC(CPI + f_{MRPI} \, t_{acci}) t_{Clock}$$

IC stands for instruction count, t_{Clock} for clock cycle time. *CPI* describes the cycles per instruction, f_{MRPI} the memory references per instruction and t_{acci} the average number of cycles necessary for a memory access (the label *i* has the value 1 if no cache is available, 2 if the system owns a level 1 cache and 3 if level 1 and level 2 caches are available). *CPU* can be calculated with the equations of the previous sections.

For *n* levels of cache we obtain the formula:

$$CPU_i = IC\left(CPI + f_{MRPI} \left(\sum_{\alpha=1}^{\alpha=n+1} t_\alpha \left(\prod_{\beta=0}^{\beta=\alpha-1} f_\beta \right) \right) \right) t_{Clock}$$

For a system with n levels of cache we can write the formula:

$$\chi_{ST} = K \sqrt{\xi\zeta \frac{WU}{VT}}$$

χ_{ST} (ST: Spacetime) representing the cache hit rate in a cache with ζ cache lines each of ξ bit length. This formula does not take the cache hierarchy into consideration!

For example in a cache system with two hierarchy levels where the level 1 cache is a subset of the bigger level 2 cache we obtain a χ_{ST1} smaller than χ_{ST2}. This is clear because a cache with more cache lines leads always to a bigger hit rate. But due to the hierarchy we must also consider that only a subset of the processor accesses to the level 1 cache also lead to an access to the level 2 cache; and this fact is not considered in the formula for χ_{ST}! For the two hierarchy system we can write:

$$\chi_{ST} = \chi_1 + \chi_2(1 - \chi_1)$$

with χ_1 and χ_2 the cache hit rate of the level 1 and level 2 cache respectively (as described in the previous sections). If we have for example 90% hit rate in the level 1 cache and 80% hit rate in the level 2 cache then we obtain a χ_{ST} of $(0,9+0,8(1-0,9))=0,98$ (98%). The 98% hit rate would occur if we would have only one cache with the size of the level 2 cache.

We can proceed now in a recursive manner. Let's assume we have calculated $\chi_{ST}=\chi_1$ in the first step. According to the equation for χ_{ST} we can write: $\chi_2 = \dfrac{\chi_{ST} - \chi_1}{1 - \chi_1}$. In a system with three levels of cache we obtain (implying now the knowledge of χ_1 and χ_2):

$$\chi_3 = \frac{\chi_{ST} - \chi_1 - \chi_2(1-\chi_1)}{(1-\chi_1)(1-\chi_2)}.$$ For n levels of cache we obtain finally:

$$\chi_n = \frac{\chi_{ST} - \chi_1 - \chi_2(1-\chi_1) - \chi_3(1-\chi_2)(1-\chi_1) - \ldots - \chi_{n-1}(1-\chi_{n-2})(1-\chi_{n-3})\ldots(1-\chi_1)}{(1-\chi_1)(1-\chi_2)(1-\chi_3)\ldots(1-\chi_{n-1})}.$$

This can be written as:

$$\chi_n = \frac{\chi_{ST} - \chi_1 - \sum_{j=2}^{j=n-1} \chi_j \prod_{i=1}^{i=j-1}(1-\chi_i)}{\prod_{i=1}^{i=n-1}(1-\chi_i)}.$$

If we introduce this formula in the formula for the CPU-time we obtain:

$$CPU_i = IC \left(CPI + f_{MRPI} \left(\sum_{\alpha=1}^{\alpha=n+1} t_\alpha \left(\prod_{\beta=0}^{\beta=\alpha-1} \left(1 - \left(\frac{K_\beta \sqrt{\xi_\beta \zeta_\beta \frac{WU}{VT}} - \chi_1 - \sum_{j=2}^{j=\beta-1} \chi_j \left(\prod_{i=1}^{i=j-1}(1-\chi_i) \right)}{\prod_{i=1}^{i=\beta-1}(1-\chi_i)} \right) \right) \right) \right) \right) t_{Clock}$$

The magnitudes W, U, V, T, ξ and ζ are described in the previous paragraphs. The χ_n are the cache hit rates of the n-th level of cache.

3.3 Speedup

The speedup of an application is given by Amdahl's law [1]:

$$Speedup = \frac{1}{1 - Percent - of - time - with - improvement + \dfrac{Percent - of - time - with - improvement}{\dfrac{CPU_{improve}}{CPU_{no-improve}}}}$$

The $Percent - of - time - with - improvement$ is in many cases 100% because the improvement (e.g. the cache) is available for the whole duration of the application. $CPU_{improve}$ represents the CPU-time in the situation where the improvement is available (e.g. the cache is active), whereas $CPU_{no-improve}$ describes the CPU-time in the situation where the improvement is not available (e.g. the cache is not active).

In most of our application types the $Percent - of - time - with - improvement$ is equal to one (100 %) because the caches are available during the whole operation time. In these cases the equation is simplified to [1]:

$$Speedup = \frac{CPU_{improve}}{CPU_{no-improve}}.$$

Bibliography

[1]: John L Hennessy, David A Patterson: Computer Architecture: A Quantitative Approach; Second Edition; Morgan Kaufmann Publishers; 1990.